IMPROVING OUR ENVIRONMENT

Saving Energy

Jen Green

GARETH STEVENS
GS
PUBLISHING
A World Almanac Education Group Company

Please visit our web site at: www.garethstevens.com
For a free color catalog describing Gareth Stevens Publishing's list of high-quality books
and multimedia programs, call 1-800-542-2595 (USA) or 1-800-387-3178 (Canada).
Gareth Stevens Publishing's fax: (414) 332-3567.

Library of Congress Cataloging-in-Publication Data

Green, Jen.
    Saving energy / Jen Green.
        p. cm. — (Improving our environment)
    Includes bibliographical references and index.
    ISBN 0-8368-4430-0 (lib. bdg.)
        1. Energy conservation—Juvenile literature.   I. Title.   II. Series.
    TJ163.35.G74   2005
    333.791'6—dc22   2004056596

This North American edition first published in 2005 by
Gareth Stevens Publishing
A World Almanac Education Group Company
330 West Olive Street, Suite 100
Milwaukee, WI 53212 USA

This U.S. edition copyright © 2005 by Gareth Stevens, Inc. Original edition copyright © 2005 by
Hodder Wayland. First published in 2005 by Hodder Wayland, an imprint of Hodder Children's Books,
a division of Hodder Headline Limited, 338 Euston Road, London NW1 3BH, U.K.

Series Editor: Victoria Brooker
Editor: Margot Richardson
Designer: Fiona Webb
Artwork: Peter Bull
Gareth Stevens Editor: Carol Ryback
Gareth Stevens Designer: Steve Schraenkler

Photo credits: CORBIS: Ted Spiegel 16; Jim Sugar 19. Ecoscene Photo Library: Rosemary Greenwood 8;
Kieran Murray 9; Visual & Written 10; Phillip Colla 25; Bruce Harber 27. Hodder Wayland Photo Library:
title page, 4; Gordon Clements 15; Christine Osborne 18; Timothy Woodcock 28; Angela Hampton 29.
Still Pictures: Jochen Tack 5; Ron Gilling 6; Julio Etchart 11; Peter Frischmuth 12; Mark Edwards 13;
Adrian Arbib 14; Shehzad Nooran 17; Jean-Francois Mutzig 20; Klaus Andrews 21; Mike Schroder 22;
Jim Wark 23; J. Vallespire/UNEP 24; Michel Coupard 26.

Printed in China

1 2 3 4 5 6 7 8 9 09 08 07 06 05

Contents

Words in **bold** can be found in the glossary.

Energy for Life

Energy is the power that makes things work. It comes in many different forms, from wind that fills a boat's sails to the fuel in a car's tank. Energy contained in muscles allows people and animals to move.

Everything we do uses energy. You've used all kinds of energy since you woke up this morning. After waking up, you used muscle energy to hop out of bed and probably switched on a light in a room heated or cooled by energy. After washing up in water that took energy to heat, you ate breakfast, which gave you energy to get yourself to school.

Animals and people move by using energy stored in their muscles. Machines run on energy from fuels. ▼

Using Energy

Every day, people use enormous amounts of energy. As the world's **population** increases, more and more energy is used. We are slowly running out of some of our main energy sources. Many of these sources also cause **pollution** that harms the environment. Everyone needs to learn to use energy wisely and carefully and not waste it.

▲ Every day, people use energy for traveling, lighting, heating or cooling, and cooking. We often take our plentiful power and fuel for granted. But our enormous demand for energy is harming the environment.

TRY THIS! **Energy Diary**

Keep track of all the energy you use in one day in an energy diary. Hot water heaters, stoves, and hair dryers all use energy. Write down every time you turn on a light, fan, stereo, television, or computer. Note whether your furnace or air conditioner is running. List what you ate to power your body. In what ways can you save energy?

Energy Sources

You may be surprised to learn that almost all energy on Earth originally came from the Sun.

Energy from Plants

Plants use **solar energy** to make their own food in a process called **photosynthesis**. In turn, plants provide people and animals with food energy. Trees use the energy in sunlight to grow thick, tall trunks. Their wood provides fuel for heating and cooking. In some parts of the world, so many trees have been cut down that firewood is scarce.

People in **developing countries** often rely on wood to provide much of their energy. In some regions, villagers have cut down all the nearby trees. They must walk a long way to gather wood. ▼

Energy Stored in the Ground

Coal, oil, and natural gas contain stored energy from the Sun. These **fossil fuels** provide countries around the world with their main sources of power. About 75 percent of the world's power comes from tapping these energy stores.

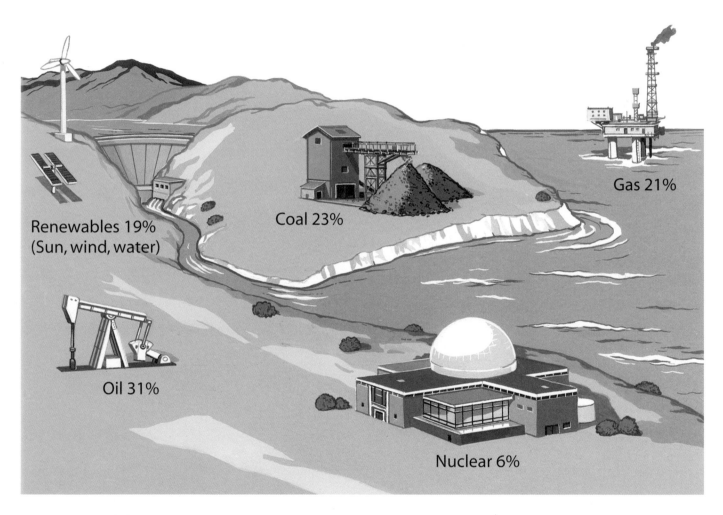

Renewables 19%
(Sun, wind, water)

Coal 23%

Gas 21%

Oil 31%

Nuclear 6%

Renewable Sources

Sunlight, wind, flowing water, and even underground hot water and rocks provide energy in some areas. These **renewable** energy sources will never run out because nature is constantly renewing or replacing them.

▲ Fossil fuels provide about 75 percent of the world's energy. Renewable sources provide another 19 percent, while **nuclear power** (*see pages 20–21*) provides the remaining 6 percent.

What Are Fossil Fuels?

Fossil fuels formed millions of years ago from the remains of plants and animals.

Coal

Black, shiny coal is formed from treelike ferns that grew in swampy forests three hundred million years ago. Many layers of soil eventually buried the dead, fallen plants. The weight of the ground squashed and heated the plants and slowly turned them into coal.

Over millions of years, heat and pressure slowly turned the remains of ancient, treelike ferns into brown, crumbly **peat** and then into coal. Many **power plants** produce energy by burning coal. ▼

◀ Oil and natural gas are mined not only on land but also at sea. Oil rigs reach deep into the ocean bed and pump up the fossil fuels that lie far beneath the waves.

Oil and Natural Gas

Oil and natural gas found beneath the oceans comes from the buried remains of **marine** animals and plants. After millions of years, the pressure of the ocean water **compresses** them, turning them into fossil fuels. Oil is the world's most important energy source. Every minute, people also burn millions of cubic feet (cubic meters) of natural gas.

TRY THIS!

Energy at Home

Make a chart of where you get the energy used in your home. What powers your furnace, stove, and electronics? Natural gas? Oil? Wood? Coal? Solar power? Wind power?

 KNOW THE FACTS

Factories called refineries process thick, black **crude oil** into many different products, including gasoline and **diesel** and airplane fuel. Oil is also a basic ingredient in a wide range of other common products, such as **synthetic** fabrics for clothing, machine parts, many types of plastic containers, eyeglass and contact lenses, and paint.

Using Fossil Fuels

Fossil fuels are valuable natural resources such as coal, oil, and natural gas. The mining of fossil fuels causes many kinds of pollution.

When coal is mined from open pits or deep tunnels, heaps of waste rock are left over. Oil wells also produce many wastes. Fossil fuels are often discovered in remote regions and must be transported over long distances for use. Supertanker ships, pipelines, and trucks carrying oil or other fuels can cause pollution if they leak their contents.

In 2002, the *Prestige* oil tanker split open off the northwest coast of Spain, spilling millions of gallons (liters) of crude oil and forming an oil slick 5 miles (8 kilometers) long. As the crude oil washed ashore, it fouled beaches and killed seabirds and other wildlife. ▼

◀ In certain crowded cities, waste gases from vehicles, high temperatures, and land formations combine to help form a poisonous haze called **smog**. This type of air pollution often wraps the tops of tall buildings in chemical clouds and hides the surrounding landscapes (in this case, Mexico City) from view.

Burning

Power plants burn fossil fuels to **generate** (produce) electricity. As the coal, oil, or natural gas is burned, it heats water to produce steam — which powers machines called **turbines**. The turbines connect to a **generator** that produces electricity. The burning of fossil fuels releases huge amounts of smoke, **soot**, and waste gases into the air.

Vehicle Fuels

Cars, trucks, planes, and other vehicles consume large amounts of fuel — about one-third of all the oil used each year worldwide. Vehicles in the United States **consume** about one-half of the oil used in the country every year.

 KNOW THE FACTS

In Asia, about 1.5 million people die each year from air pollution-related illnesses caused by wastes from cars, trucks, and buses.

Worldwide Energy Use

People in different parts of the world use very different amounts of energy. People in **developed countries**, such as the United States, Canada, and Japan, use far more energy than people in developing countries such as Ecuador or Ethiopia.

Developed Countries

Most people in developed countries seldom think about their daily energy use. Appliances such as microwaves, vacuum cleaners, and dishwashers may make life easier, but they guzzle fuel. Only about 25 percent of the world's population consumes about 70 percent of its energy.

▲ Lights in shops, stores, and offices often blaze all night in larger cities such as Seattle, Washington. This practice wastes enormous amounts of energy.

Developing Countries

People in developing countries own fewer cars and other machines, so they use far less energy. Instead of using just fossil fuels, they also burn wood, animal **dung**, or crop waste for heating and cooking. But populations in many developing countries are increasing rapidly, and people there also want the machines that make life more comfortable. Fossil fuel use is rising in developing countries.

When wood is scarce in developing countries, people sometimes burn animal dung instead. This Indian woman is drying dung to use as fuel. ▼

Saving Energy

People in developed countries can save precious energy in hundreds of ways. For example, we could walk more or ride the bus, wear sweaters rather than turning up the heat, and wash only full loads of clothing using cold water instead of hot water.

Running Low

One hundred years ago, it seemed as if fossil fuels would last forever. At the current rate of use, some fossil fuels, such as oil and natural gas, may only last another century or so.

◀ Many Middle Eastern countries, including Saudia Arabia and Kuwait, hold the world's largest oil reserves. In the last fifty years, selling oil abroad has made some of these countries wealthy.

 KNOW THE FACTS

Earth's oil and natural gas reserves may last fewer than one hundred years. Coal stocks will probably last another two or three centuries, but eventually they will run out, too.

Nonrenewable

Coal, oil, and natural gas took millions of years to form through processes that cannot be copied. These fossil fuels are considered sources of **nonrenewable** energy because they cannot be replaced after use.

Burning Oil

Every year, as the world's population increases, the use of fossil fuels increases, especially in developing countries. As more people can afford to buy refrigerators, cars, and electronics, more factories open to supply them with goods. These increases in industrial production put a greater demand on power plants that produce energy by burning fossil fuels, especially oil.

▲ China is an enormous developing country. Even though it has many large, modern cities, most of its workers ride bikes instead of driving cars. Many farmers and people in rural areas still use animals for power and transportation.

Pollution Problems

Pollution is another problem related to fossil fuel use. Coal, oil, and natural gas release waste gases as they burn. As these gases build up, they can change the world's climate and cause yet another serious problem — **acid rain**.

Acid Rain

Gases released by vehicles, power plants, and factories as they burn coal, oil, and natural gas mix with **water vapor** in the air to make rain that contains a weak acid. Acid rain harms trees, runs into rivers and lakes, and kills water life.

A scientist samples water at Woods Lake in New York during the spring melt. Data on the effects of acid rain on the lake should help researchers determine how to counteract the problem. ▼

Global Warming

Carbon dioxide, **methane**, and other gases found in Earth's atmosphere warm and protect the planet's surface. But the burning of fossil fuels adds extra amounts of these gases to the atmosphere, causing a **greenhouse effect** — which changes the climate and increases **global warming**. Some dry areas become drier, while others receive more rain, sleet, or snow. An increase in the average temperature of oceans causes faster melting of the polar ice caps, and worldwide sea levels rise. Low areas flood more frequently.

▲ The low-lying country of Bangladesh in Asia has experienced frequent, severe flooding in recent years. Scientists fear that global warming will cause increased flooding in other areas around the globe.

TRY THIS!

Explore the Greenhouse Effect

Solar heat combines with atmospheric gases to trap heat near Earth's surface — much like the glass roof and walls that trap hot air inside a greenhouse. See for yourself how this works. Put a thermometer in sunlight for ten minutes and record the temperature. Next, seal the thermometer inside a clear glass jar and set it in sunlight for ten minutes. Are the temperatures the same or different? Why?

Fossil Fuel Crisis

The enormous amounts of fossil fuel burned every day pollute the environment with harmful wastes. As fossil fuel supplies run out, people must take action to reduce fossil fuel use, cut pollution, and save energy.

Tackling the Energy Crisis

Everyone must cut fossil fuel use to keep the energy crisis from getting worse. Fossil fuel supplies will last longer with careful use. Design changes in the different ways that industries, vehicles, machines, and power plants burn fossil fuels will cause less pollution. Research and development into methods of fossil fuel use that save energy will also help.

▲ Buses, trains, and other forms of public transportation lessen the need for private cars. An efficient streetcar system that runs through Amsterdam, the Netherlands, reduces pollution, traffic problems, and fossil fuel use.

▲ The enormous task of cleaning up after the very serious Chernobyl nuclear plant disaster presented special problems. Workers wore exposure suits and breathed through air canisters to protect themselves from the dangerous radiation and contaminated air.

A Dangerous Fuel?

In 1956, the world's first **nuclear reactor** opened in northwest Britain. Many people believed that nuclear energy offered an almost unlimited supply of safe, cheap power. Hundreds more nuclear power stations opened throughout the world over the following thirty years. Then in 1986, one of the nuclear reactors at Chernobyl in Ukraine exploded, showering deadly radiation over much of Europe. Some countries have decided to shut down their nuclear power plants because of the possible dangers.

 KNOW THE FACTS

A cloud of radiation immediately spread from the Chernobyl accident site, and within weeks, about 1,900 square miles (5,000 square kilometers) of land around the plant was declared unsafe. Residents moved away. Radiation released by the disaster may have killed up to ten thousand people since 1986.

Sunlight and Water Energy

Sunlight and flowing water contain energy that can generate electricity. These renewable energy sources cause much less harm to the environment than fossil fuels do.

Solar Energy

The Sun's energy can be captured in various ways. Solar panels trap heat that generates electricity, heats water, and warms houses. Solar power will not run out and causes no pollution but works best in very sunny areas. Although solar-powered equipment is expensive to build, people save money in the long run because they spend less on other types of fuel, such as oil or natural gas, over the years.

Solar panels must face the Sun to work efficiently. This solar-powered house is in Germany. ▼

▲ **When this dam in Utah was built, it flooded the land behind it and formed a reservoir. Sometimes, entire towns must relocate to avoid the area to be flooded.**

Water Power

Water flowing downhill contains energy. For thousands of years, people have used water energy to drive machines such as mill wheels. Modern power plants on or near dams produce electricity using fast-flowing water. A dam changes the landscape behind it to form an enormous lake, called a reservoir, that holds a ready supply of water to harness for power. Water spins turbines attached to generators that change the water's energy into electricity. Energy produced by flowing water is called **hydroelectric power** (**HEP**).

 KNOW THE FACTS

Hydroelectric power produces 90 percent of all electricity generated by renewable resources. The United States uses HEP to produce nearly 10 percent of its electricity. Every day, HEP provides about 20 percent of the world's electricity needs.

Wind and Hot Rocks

Electricity generated by renewable sources, such as wind power and **geothermal power**, is considered "clean" or nonpolluting energy. Geothermal power — heat energy produced deep within the Earth — heats rock layers and can turn groundwater into steam.

Geothermal Energy

In some volcanic regions, such as Iceland and New Zealand, hot rocks lie close to Earth's surface. A geothermal power plant generates electricity from the steam produced by piping cold water through the hot rocks. In most other volcanic areas, the hot rocks lie too far below the surface to provide a convenient source of geothermal power.

▲ Hot springs that bubble up from beneath Iceland provide recreational areas. Geothermal power plants use the hot water to produce electricity.

24

▲ Wind farms, such as this one near Palm Springs, California, contain many rows of tall wind turbines (high-tech windmills) that produce electricity using renewable wind energy.

Wind Energy

Wind turbines are tall, streamlined versions of the windmills that dotted farms and countrysides in past centuries. A collection of many wind turbines linked to a set of electric generators is called a wind farm. As wind spins the turbine blades, electricity flows to nearby homes and businesses. Some people say wind farms spoil their view.

 KNOW THE FACTS

The Wairakei geothermal plant in New Zealand generates about 10 percent of that country's electricity. In the United States, wind energy provides power for one million people.

New Energy Sources

Researchers are developing new, low-pollution energy sources. Future energy needs will probably rely on a wide range of power sources.

Energy from the Oceans

Ocean **tides** produce energy from changing water levels. Large floating containers called "nodding ducks" provide power by harnessing wave energy. As the ducks rock with the waves, they spin turbines that generate electricity. A barrier called a **barrage** built across a river mouth traps water at high tide and uses it to spin turbines as the tide falls. Tidal energy only produces one or two bursts of energy a day because there are only one or two high tides per day.

A barrage on the Rance River in northern France contains a tidal power plant that has been generating electricity since the 1960s. The barrage doubles as a bridge. ▼

Energy for the Future

Special **incinerators** generate power by burning garbage. One of the drawbacks is that the fires must burn at extremely high temperatures to prevent the escape of poisonous gases. Another possible fuel source of the future involves a type of nuclear energy called fusion, which uses **hydrogen** as fuel. Although the world will never run out of hydrogen, power generated by nuclear fusion is difficult to control.

▲ Filters inside the chimney of a modern power plant reduce the amounts of harmful gases released into the air.

 KNOW THE FACTS

North Americans use more energy per person than people in any other region. Australians, Europeans, Russians, and the Japanese also use a lot of energy. People in Africa and rural China use the least energy.

HELPING OUT **Energy-Saving Lightbulbs**

Energy-saving lightbulbs cost more than ordinary lightbulbs, but they produce the same amount of light, last much longer, and use only about one-fifth as much power.

Get Involved!

Every day, people around the world can save energy by cutting back in some small way on their daily need for power. This action by all will save an enormous amount of resources.

Simple steps for saving energy include switching off lights and turning off electronic equipment such as flat-screen televisions and computers after use. Cold weather increases energy use in homes. A well-**insulated** home uses less fuel for heating and reduces monthly costs. Ask home owners to repair or replace drafty doors and windows. Wear a sweater and turn down the thermostat a few degrees to cut energy use. In warm seasons, wear lighter clothing and open windows to let in a breeze or set the air conditioning temperature a degree or two warmer.

◄ **Save energy on nice days by drying clothing outside instead of using an electric or gas dryer.**

Cycle and Recycle

Every family can save energy by planning errands wisely and using public transportation whenever possible. Students can help by walking, riding bikes, taking the school bus, or asking parents to set up a car pool with others in their neighborhood to get to school. Recycle aluminum cans, plastic, and newspapers instead of throwing them away.

HELPING OUT — Stop an Energy Drain

A television, stereo, DVD player, or any other device that uses a remote control places a small but constant drain on energy sources. How can you solve this problem?

▲ If possible, walk to the grocery store instead of driving there. It's a good way to exercise, and it saves money, too.

Glossary

acid rain rain made acidic by pollution.

barrage a barrier built across moving water to form a dam or to divert the water.

carbon dioxide a gas that is naturally present in the atmosphere but is also produced as a waste gas when anything is burned and when living organisms breathe.

compresses squashes under pressure.

consume to use up.

crude oil unprocessed petroleum.

developed countries richer countries with well-developed industries.

developing countries poorer countries with less well-developed industries.

diesel a syrupy, oil-based fuel, commonly used in buses, trucks, and heavy machinery that emits solid and gaseous wastes.

dung animal waste; manure.

fossil fuels fuels, such as coal, oil, and natural gas, that formed from the fossilized remains of plants and animals.

generate to make or produce.

generator a machine that produces electricity from mechanical energy.

geothermal power a type of renewable energy produced by nuclear reactions deep within Earth's hot inner core that cause water to bubble up to the surface in the form of steam, hot pools, or geysers and that can be tapped to provide power.

global warming the worldwide rise in average annual temperatures caused by human-made pollution and some natural disasters, such as erupting volcanoes.

greenhouse effect the gradual increase in the amounts of gases trapped in Earth's atmosphere caused by the worldwide burning of fossil fuels.

hybrid vehicles vehicles that can run on two different power sources.

hydroelectric power (HEP) electricity generated by flowing water.

hydrogen a highly flammable (burnable), odorless, tasteless, and colorless gas commonly found in the atmosphere.

incinerators industrial ovens that burn garbage to ashes.

insulated kept warm by materials that prevent heat from escaping.

marine belonging or related to saltwater.

methane a colorless, odorless, flammable greenhouse gas produced by burning certain fuels and when once-living matter decays.

nonrenewable unable to be replaced.

nuclear power energy released by splitting tiny particles called atoms.

nuclear reactor a type of power generator that produces energy by splitting atoms.

oil slick a floating layer of oil on the surface of water that can coat and poison animals and sea life and that often washes ashore to soil the coastline.

peat layers of dead plants that pile up in water and partially rot.

photosynthesis the process plants use to make food using sunlight, water, and carbon dioxide gas.

pollution the results of harmful substances that damage the environment.

power plants factories that produce electricity, usually by burning fossil fuels.

population all the things that live in a particular area.

radiation invisible, often harmful rays given off by the Sun or nuclear reactions.

renewable replaceable.

reservoir a large lake made by damming a river. Reservoirs are often used for recreation and as sources of water power.

smog a poisonous haze caused by exhaust fumes mixing with hot, humid, stationary air masses.

solar energy power produced from sunlight.

soot a fine black powder released into the air when coal or wood is burned.

synthetic made by people.

tides the usually twice-daily rise and fall of the water levels in oceans and connected bodies of water.

turbines machines powered by steam, natural gas, or water that spin a set of blades connected to a shaft that turns to generate electricity.

water vapor water in the air in the form of a colorless gas.

Further Information

Books

Alternative Energy. True Books (series). Christine Petersen (Children's Press)

Alternative Energy Sources. Science at the Edge (series). Sally Morgan (Heinemann)

Biofuel Power of the Future: New Ways of Turning Organic Matter into Energy. The Library of Future Energy (series). Chris Hayhurst (Rosen)

Energy: Coal. Nuclear Energy. Oil & Gas. Solar Power. Water Power. Wind Power. Science Files (series). Steve Parker (Gareth Stevens)

Energy Resources: Our Impact on the Planet. 21st Century Debates (series). Ewan McLeish (Steck-Vaughn)

Earth's Resources. Science Fact Files (series). Steve Parker (Raintree)

Energy for Life (series). Robert Snedden (Heinemann Library)

Global Pollution. Face the Facts (series). Paul Brown (Heinemann)

Global Warming: The Threat of Earth's Changing Climate. Laurence Pringle (SeaStar Books)

Saving Energy Web Sites

Dr. E's Energy Lab
www.eere.energy.gov/kids/

Energy Quest
www.energyquest.ca.gov/index.html

Energy Saving Tips for Schools
www.ase.org/content/article/detail/625

How Can You Save Energy?
www.tvakids.com/electricity/conservation.htm

Powerhouse Kids — Saving Energy
www.powerhousekids.com/savingenergy/renewable.php

Rocky Mountain Institute for Kids — Energy
www.rmi.org/sitepages/pid479.php

Saving Energy
www.energyquest.ca.gov/saving_energy/

U.S. Department of Energy — Kids Zone
www.energy.gov/engine/content.do?BT_CODE=KIDS

Index

Numbers in **bold** refer to illustrations.